tulips and forget-me-nots

bela h

also from Bela H:

healing my heart

chapters

the unconditional love 9
the ache 57
the healing 105
dear stranger 168
dear me 169

dedication

to all the broken hearts that need mending

i wish i had gotten all the flowers you promised me. i wish i had gotten tulips and forget-me-nots as a symbol of your love. you probably don't even remember my favourite flower, the lilac. but i won't talk here about all the flowers i've never gotten and all the promises you haven't kept. i'll talk about the way i loved you and the way you hurt me and the way you forced me to heal from the only person i've never wanted to have to heal from. i'll talk about you here and how you broke my heart.

i went through so many emotions after you left me. sadness, anger, disappointment, fear, guilt, hope, grief. i felt the ache to the fullest. i spent days not eating and nights not sleeping, crying my eyes out in my pillows. i thought that my life ended here, that i wouldn't find anyone else to love me and that i wouldn't find anyone else to love as much as i loved you.

but this is the thing with heartbreaks. we give our all to a person we think will stay forever, and feel lost the moment they exit our lives. they force us into an emotional rollercoaster, in which it seems like we only have bad days and in which the fear and adrenaline kick in to their fullest. we want it to end the moment it starts and are afraid to take it as a possibility to grow, because what if all of our fears become reality? what if there isn't another person after them?

but the truth is that we should take it as an opportunity to evolve and become a better version of ourselves. it sounds so cliché, i know, but would not doing anything and drowning yourself in hope and grief make you feel any better? it didn't work for me at least.

it's a long way, the healing journey after a heartbreak. for me it felt like i had to heal from trauma, and you may be feeling the same. the worst thing is that you will have to do the hard work yourself. and it will hurt, it probably will for a long time. you have a big heart and you gave your all, and when that person left, they took it with them. but you can love again. that love you gave them, it is still within you.

i hope you can find yourself in these pages that reflect the feelings i went through. it proves you are not alone and that there will always be light at the end of the tunnel.

the unconditional love

do i still love him?
i don't know
i've asked myself this question numerous times
wondering whether you deserve my love
calculating every possibility in my head
dreaming about scenarios
which may lead to you
possibly loving me, too

but what is love?
i think it's more than just butterflies
i think it's the feeling of safety
that i feel when i'm in your arms
i think it's the feeling of home
knowing that you found your place
the feeling of knowing you're not alone
and that you have someone's gaze

so maybe i do still love you
even if i wish i didn't
and maybe you do love me, too
even if you'll never admit it

thinking about you
sends shivers down my spine
i loved you unconditionally
wholeheartedly calling you mine
i loved everything about you
but what was there not to love
you were everything that i've ever wanted
my dream come true
and my glimpse of hope

i don't think
that i'll ever lose feelings for you
you meant too much
i fell too hard
and i am certain
that the curtains weren't supposed
to close on our love story yet

that's why
i'll never lose feelings for you
because there may always be a way
to raise those curtains up again
and ignite the flame of our love once more
that we never wanted to blow out

my mind
is a prison of my thoughts
and you are the inmate

i can't stop thinking about you

your name
is my favourite word
your voice
is my favourite sound
your eyes
are my favourite mirror
your arms
are my favourite place
your love
is my favourite feeling

i adore you too much

there will never be enough words
in the english language
to describe the feelings
that i get when i'm with you

the butterflies i feel flying
whenever i look at you
the chills i get
when i only think of you
the unconscious smile i have on my face
whenever i imagine us together

with you, everything was different
and not in a cringe kind of way
or a 'everyone says that' kind of way

you were truly different than anyone i've
ever met before you. i was different around
you, in a better way. it was with you when i
laughed and loved the hardest. you gave love
a whole new meaning and i'll be forever
grateful for that, for letting me experience
such intense emotions.

with you it was different the moment our
story started. there were no games, no lies,
no second-guessing. i found my home when
i found you, the place where i wanted to
stay forever. i found the person i wanted to
share 63000 meals with throughout my life,
the person i wanted to tell 21000 times about
my day, the person i wanted to hold in my
arms when i fell asleep and woke up to in
the morning.

when i met you, my heart instantly chose
yours, without asking me first. it finally
found its soulmate.

tulips and forget-me-nots

loving you
always warmed up my heart
it always left me going to sleep
with an enormous smile on my face
and waking up to another
thinking about you

i never planned to fall in love with you. meeting you came out of nowhere, and i remember from the beginning it felt like i had known you forever. you made everything feel so easy and you made my empty heart bloom with a garden full of flowers. i didn't want to fall in love when i met you, but your charm was making my knees weak. so i fell for you, harder than someone ever could, bruising my knees along the way and scraping my entire heart during the process.

but falling in love with you was worth all the bruises and all the scrapes.

i chose you
when i first started talking to you
i chose to let you in my life
to give you a glimpse of my world
i chose you for so many firsts
thinking you'd also be part of all my lasts
i chose to be vulnerable with you
to open up to you more than i did to anyone

i kept choosing you
year after year
keeping my pinky promise of forever

how i wish that you'd have chosen me too
keeping *your* pinky promise of forever

i'm a hopeless romantic
always thinking that true love finds its way
sooner or later
believing in love at first sight
because i'm pretty sure that's what i felt
when i first saw you
because i'm pretty sure that's what you felt
when you first saw me
almost dropping your coffee, remember?

i'm a hopeless romantic
thinking that we all have our soulmate
and that you surely are mine
that our souls are somewhat connected
and somehow mine will find its way
back to yours
that both our hearts collided for a reason

i'm a hopeless romantic
who will never stop believing in love
and who will never give up on loving
and being loved back

maybe i just love the way everything feels so familiar with you. the way loving you seems like the easiest task to complete, because i've been doing it for so long. maybe i just got used to wanting you every day. maybe i still love you, because it's the only thing i know. maybe it's the security that i crave so much in my life that keeps me so attached to you.

but if loving you feels so easy, doesn't that mean that i'm destined to do it?

if you had asked me to
i'd have taken all the stars from the night sky
and given them to you
i'd have crossed oceans
just to make you happy
i'd have have given you everything
in a heartbeat
just to see you smile
i'd have done so much for you
without even expecting anything in return

- *things people do in the name of love*

sometimes
when i lay alone at night
i still imagine your arms wrapped around me
embracing my body and soul
you whispering softly in my ear
i still imagine your hands on my body
the soft touch of your fingertips
it still gives me shivers
whenever i imagine you next to me

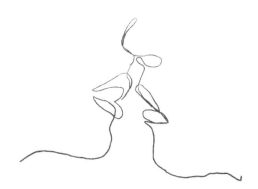

i think you were the only person
who never told me that i'm boring
the only person
who laughed at my stupid jokes for hours
the only person
who was interested in my thoughts
and feelings
the only person
who truly loved hearing about my day
about the little things that happened to me
as insignificant as they might have been
the only person
who genuinely understood me
and with whom i felt safe with

now i'm looking for you in every new person i meet

when people ask me about you
i longingly remember
all the love that we shared
i have to chuckle
because i recall the ways
you've made me laugh
but then it also hits me
that now i have to live with the ghost of you
and my eyes get uncontrollably teary, too
all i can bring out of my mouth is
'he probably was the love of my life
and the story i never wanted to end'

my heart
will never forget you completely
i'll never forget the times you made me laugh
until i had tears in my eyes
i'll never forget the feeling of safety you gave me
whenever you held me tightly in your arms
kissing my head and caressing my hair
i'll never forget the way you looked at me
as if i was the only girl in the world
i'll never forget the sound of your heartbeat
whenever i laid my head on your chest

you'll always have a part of my heart
even if it's just a small fragment of it

i wish i could fall in love with myself
the way i fell in love with you

what i loved the most about you were the little things you did. how you could never leave the house without your headphones. how you could never go a day without having a snack at 5 p.m. how it took you ages to get in the shower, and once you did you wouldn't come out for so long. the way you couldn't get out of bed for at least ten minutes, unless i was drowning your face in little kisses.

but isn't this what love is about?
the little things a person does
that may seem so insignificant to outsiders
but to you, those things mean everything
they're the reason
you fell in love with that person
the reason
you continue to be in love with them
the reason
you can't forget them

i still remember
how everyone envied the way you looked at me
and the genuine happiness we felt
whenever we were together
how everyone told us
you make a beautiful couple
and if you ever break up
i'll stop believing in love
how since we broke up
people tell me that true love like ours
doesn't just disappear
and that we just need time for ourselves
to find our way back to each other

but i miss expressing my love
i miss being the reason for your smile
i miss listening to our songs
and looking at our pictures
i miss being yours
and i miss calling you mine
i miss my best friend
and i miss my partner in crime

how much longer until you're back into my arms?

a part of me
will always be missing

it will always belong to you

there's nothing
that i want more
than to be able to go back in time
before things started to crumble
and fall apart
to go back in time
to finish what we started
to fill the cracks in our story
with more love and desire
to save what's left to save
and to put out the fire
that we accidentally started

lie to me once more
let's spend the night
under a sky full of stars
and lie about the way we still want each other

hold me in your arms once more
like we've never had history
like we've just met for the first time
let me feel your heartbeat next to mine

kiss me one last time
let me feel the touch of your lips on mine
whisper one last 'i love you'
and tell me you are lucky to have me in your life

you say that you don't want to lose me
but you're not doing anything to keep me
you say that you don't want to hurt me
but you're not doing anything to protect me
you say that you miss me
but whenever my phone rings
it's never your name on my screen

so many sweet words
and so many sweet lies

take your time

heal. mature. grow. become a better person. do everything that i am holding you back from.

take your time

and when you're ready
the door may still be cracked open
since you didn't close it completely
when you left

i made sure to keep it unlocked

i guess the only thing that i can do now
is love you from afar
it feels like a big gray cloud hanging over me
and your memories feel like a scar

i was absolutely crazy for you
and i believed that you were too
i thought that something like ours
so unique and magical
would last a lifetime
would last forever

you promised me a lifetime
you promised me forever
you promised
and i really thought you meant it

but now i'm left with empty promises
a lifetime i'm not looking forward to
and a forever that only existed in my head

do you think
that it would have been possible
to learn how to love myself
while staying by your side
and love you too?

i miss
hearing that you love me
your hand placed gently on my face
as you look deeply into my eyes
lean down and kiss me on the lips
from time to time
i can still feel you doing that
but i know it's too surreal
and i'll never experience it again
not with you

that's not how i wanted this to end

and when you meet me, please try to truly know me, the real me, who only opens up to a few people. and when you choose me, please handle my heart with care. it has way too many scars and blisters, and i don't know how much more it can bear. and when you love me, please love me unconditionally. please think of me as someone, who you would never risk losing. please try to look deep into the core of my heart, where i keep all the endless love that i have for everyone. and if you really have to, please don't forget me when you leave me. please remember me as someone, who would have fought for you, no matter how hard the situation may have been.

please remember me as the person, who would have adored you forever.

petals
falling on the ground
one by one
getting blown away by the wind
as i am trying to figure out
if you might still love me
asking the universe for a sign

i ran out of daisies and you're still gone

almost forever, that's what we were. almost what we both needed. almost enough love to keep us together. almost happy together. you almost kept loving me like i did.

always an *almost*, but never an *enough*.

my heart
has such an endless amount of love to give
and i mean it
when i say it's unconditional
it's impossible for me
to unlove people i once loved passionately
to unlove people i wanted in my life forever

my heart
breaks very easily
because it always loves more
than another person's heart loves it back
the unconditional love
never gets reciprocated
the way it should

my heart
never gets taken care of
the way it takes care of everybody else's
but when i met you
i saw a glimmer of hope
that maybe your heart would take care of mine
i never thought that i could be so wrong

i've always dreamt of a perfect love. a love we only see in movies, with a perfect happy ending, in which two people do anything to end up together. a love that despite difficult circumstances survives everything, no matter what. a love that never leaves you second-guessing, that never ceases.

i thought that we had that love. i believe that part of me still thinks that we did and that we will have it again. maybe i'm delusional, but you're the person that i still want to love. now, in a week, in a month and in a decade. i still want to love you forever and longer, unconditionally.

where did we go wrong?
when did our paths
suddenly change direction?
why can't you be here
laying with me
telling me the same stupid jokes
that i've already heard a thousand times?
why can't i feel the warmth
of being in your arms?

i miss you, please come back

we could have been forever
you know that?
we could have had
endless kitchen dances
neverending tickling competitions
daily laughters and kisses
you could have been with someone
who would have never left your side
you could have been with someone
who had unconditional love for you
you could have had it all
and you decided that you were better off
having nothing

i wonder
if you ever loved me
as much as you claimed you did
if part of you
still wanted to fight and stick around

maybe you were torn in-between
maybe you were doubting if you should leave
maybe it was just too much
and your heart couldn't handle it anymore

and i get it
i'm hard to love
i'm a mess and overthink non-stop
i'm hard to handle
i get upset fast
and i must feel like a burden sometimes
at least that's how i perceive it in my head

but my love is pure
my love is lighthearted
it never discontinues
nor ceases during hard times

my love is unconditional
my love is a one of a kind
my love is a once in a lifetime chance
and something that from now on you'll lack

the loneliest feeling in the world
is loving someone
who doesn't want to love you
with the same intensity back

i gave my heart away and haven't seen it since

7 years -
that's how long it will take my skin
to not have felt your touch
for all the cells to recover
and to erase the imprints
that your fingers left on me

but it won't be enough time
to forget you
and everything that you've meant to me

i'm trying to understand, i swear i am. i'm trying to understand why you would leave a person who loves you with all her heart. i really am trying to understand how it can be so easy to let go of what we once had, of our beautiful love story. i am trying really hard to understand your indifference, and why you seem so unaffected by it. maybe you're hiding your pain, maybe you're acting like you're fine, while in reality you're actually hurting just like me.

i wish you would tell me that i'm wrong. i wish that i could hear my doorbell ring, and see you outside my apartment, just for you to tell me that all this isn't true. that you're not unaffected, that you're not fine and that you miss me to death. i wish i could hear those three words that i haven't heard in so long from you.

but until then, i guess i will have to keep trying to understand you. to find excuses and explanations, and tiptoe around the elephant in the room. to make up scenarios in my head and to come up with my own answers, reinventing our whole story.

- *unbearable silence*

all my friends
are telling me to stop loving you
to let you go and move on

but they don't know anything about us
they don't know about the sleepless nights
that we spent dreaming about our future

they don't know about my laughter
that truly came to light
whenever i was with you

they don't know about the times
you held me in your arms
and picked me up when i fell

they don't know about the way i felt
when i first met you
when i knew that it was you all along

they don't know anything about us
and they don't know
that it's impossible
to let you go and move on

i dreamt about you last night. i almost forgot what it felt like, because you haven't visited me too often in my sleep lately. i didn't even think that my mind would remember your face. but it was spring, the flowers were blooming and you came over to my house to meet me. you hugged me tightly, kissed me on the cheek and told me that you still want me. we started over, doing it right this time, loving each other once more. i still see your face so vividly in front of me, your eyes staring at mine full of love. your dimples coming to light because of the huge smile that you have on your face. your curls messy, as they usually are, falling on your forehead.

it felt like home
but too good to be true
and it made me wonder
if you ever dream about me, too

i hate that i still love you
and can't get you out of my head
i hate that i still wish to hear from you
just in case you want us back
i hate that i still want to be with you
after everything you've done
i hate that i can still imagine us two together
and want to keep you in my heart
i hate that i can't get over the fact
that you're not mine anymore
and i hate that i still crave you
after you broke my heart

but what i hate the most is
the way that i can't hate you

right person wrong time. that's what i'm telling myself since you left. but somehow it feels so pathetic, so pointless. if you were the right person, it would work, no? the right person would fight for me, no? you wouldn't wait for the right time, because the timing might never be right. that's why it's maybe just an excuse to not admit that the relationship failed. you think that it would work, just not right now. that you're meant to be together, but not at this moment in time. that the love is still there, but you both need to heal from your past first and you simply can't do that together.

but maybe you were the right person at the right time. you came into my life to show me that i can be loved and that i'm worth it. you came into my life when i least expected it, when i needed someone like you more than anything else. i still hope that i'm wrong and that it's truly not our time yet. that we'll both meet each other again, under the same unexpected circumstances, when we're both ready and try again.

and that next time, we'll do it right.

i don't think
that we were supposed to end like this
to not have our happy ending
to not finish writing our story
to run out of ink
right before the huge plot twist

and i think you know that
i think you are trying
to blur it out of your mind
to hide from your feelings
to find a hideout
and to disappear from reality for a little while

tulips and forget-me-nots

in another lifetime
i hope i get the chance
to love you again
without it hurting my heart

i hope that in another lifetime
we'll share bedsheets
and cuddle as we go to sleep

i hope that in another lifetime
my nights won't feel as lonely
because i'll spend them with you
laughing and dancing again in the kitchen

in another lifetime
i hope that a kiss from you starts my day
and another one ends it

i really hope
that as the earth turns around every day
you'll turn around, too
and find your way back to me

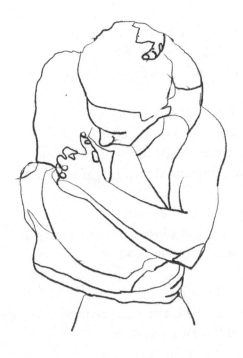

the ache

we planted a seed when we first met
in our little garden of love
we cared for it for some time
watering it every day
with patience and passion
letting the shine of our laughter
keep it warm

it grew for a while
into a beautiful blossom tree
until one october day
blew all the flowers away
the winter worsened the situation
and the once unconditional adoration
couldn't stop the withering
of our beautiful blossom tree

tulips and forget-me-nots

my heart was shattered out of nowhere
and i saw no way out
no way out to stitch it back together

i thought that i needed to rely on others
to help me put the pieces back in place
believing that i was too weak to do it myself

but no one was there
and i knew that it couldn't stay broken forever

when i came to that realization
i made a pact with myself

never will i ever rely again on anyone
for my own happiness

sleepless nights
no appetite
countless tears
running down my cheeks
dwelling on
what i did wrong
manifesting
that you will come back

i didn't expect heartbreak to feel like this

tulips and forget-me-nots

it's been countless days and nights
since i can't stop crying
everything reminds me of you
every song reminds me of us dancing
every scent of your smell
every star i see
of your eyes sparkling
every person i smile at
of your lips smiling back at me
you're anchored in my heart
so heavily
and i can't get you out of it

i stopped sending paragraphs
expressing my emotions
professing my feelings
because you never understood
you never validated them

you never understood
that your words cut deeper in my skin
than a knife ever could

that every time
you didn't acknowledge them
a part of me broke

and you never will
you'll never comprehend
the pain you've put me through

my heart will never feel whole again

my biggest fear
has always been loving someone
so hard and so intensely
not being able to imagine
a future without them
a life without them
while realizing
that i don't mean the same to them
and that they are slowly falling out of love
watching that spark fade away
and not being able to do anything about it
but pray and hope
that everything will miraculously come back

my biggest fear became reality

i'm a person who wears her heart on her sleeve. who opens it to anyone who may dare to love it, despite the risk of having it broken again. i give my heart to countless people, in the hope that one of them will eventually keep it and care for it. i let people in, despite believing that they'll leave me someday and take a piece of my heart with them on their way out. maybe it would be better to lock it up and throw the key on the other side of the world.

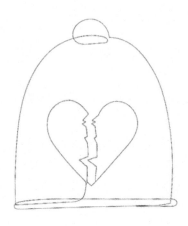

tulips and forget-me-nots

i'm scared of giving my heart
because the person i trusted the most
ripped it all apart

i'm sick
of trusting people with my soul
for repeating myself
for proving my worth
i'm sick
of people coming into my life
just to see them leave again
fading away like the sun at dusk

i need someone
who doesn't leave after the first try
who i can call at 4 a.m.
and doesn't hesitate to pick up
who notices that i'm not fine
that my eyes and cheeks are a bit too reddish
and that my words tremble
when i speak them out loud

i need someone
who comes rushing
even if it's just to keep me company
even if we only spend time in loud silence

but somehow
i keep meeting people
who feel like the touch of stinging nettle
with poison ivy on their tongues
only pretending
becoming venomous snakes
when i turn my back around

be careful with the people you let into your life

somehow it seems
like i keep getting heartbroken
making the same mistakes
over and over again
going through unendurable pain
so i'm trying to run and hide from it
run and hide from the aching
but my hideaways are uncovered
and my legs force me to run in circles

i finally end up in the same spot that i left
with the same people
that break my heart once again

sometimes i wonder if it hurts you too
whenever you think about me
if you get that little sting in your chest
whenever i cross your mind

but then i realize
that i'm probably not even worth your thought
and that you'll never know
what true agony really feels like

pinky promises in vain
had you cross your fingers again
whenever you said 'i love you'
did you think about the everlasting pain?

i crave closeness
more than anything else
i crave being held
by someone who can tell me
that everything will be alright
and that i'm safe with them
i crave being truly happy
and enjoying life to its fullest
with you by my side

disappointed
i think that's the word
that best describes how you've made me feel
disappointed
because i longed for a future with you
more than i should have
disappointed
because i believed we had a real chance
to grow old together
disappointment
is what i'm left with
and the memories of you
and the memories of us

tulips and forget-me-nots

you always told me
that you're so scared of losing me
and that you could never live without me

now look at you
choosing to face your biggest fears
losing me
and living without me

i'm tired
of half-hearted love
the type of love
that hurts you deeply
you give someone your entire being
and they take it away
without giving you anything in return

i'm not sure if true love will ever find me. i'm not sure if parts of me are lovable, if i even deserve love. i don't know if someone is able and willing to put in the effort for me. there are days when i think that i deserve to get the most meaningful love ever, but there are also days when i believe that others deserve it more.

and up to this day
i still don't understand
what i am for you

you give me hope
but at the same time take it away from me
you fill me with joy
that gets overshadowed by sorrow
and by regret
it's unexplainable
how a person can achieve that
it's unexplainable
how after so much time
you can still mess with my mind like that

tulips and forget-me-nots

and somewhere
between love and hate
our story was written

sometimes
i wish i had somebody
who really cares about me
who notices that i'm just pretending
who notices that my eyes
don't have the same spark
as they once used to
who notices my fake smile
that i use to not break down crying
i wish i had somebody
who would simply listen to me
who would understand me
even when i don't say a word
i wish i had somebody

am i stupid for still having a part of me love you? am i stupid for still hoping that you'll change your attitude, come back and start treating me right? stupid for thinking that you'll mature and want me badly enough to move mountains for me? am i stupid for desperately wanting you to be that special somebody for me?

- you can't shape someone into a person they're not

we are knee-deep in water
trying not to drown
holding tight on to each other
although we know our love
ran out of time

everything that has happened between us
has led to me having a heart
surrounded by thorns
i'm scared of letting someone in again
scared of giving someone else my all

what if they leave again?
what if i'm not good enough?
am i the only one to blame
or was it in reality not even my fault?

i'm very vulnerable
touch me and i break
my heart has many fingerprints on it
many traces that people left behind
each one of them
touched it a little bit too hard
letting it crumble
and fall apart

my mind is a mess
my thoughts all around the place
my heart screams for love
and for another heart to embrace

but who would love
such a messy mind
such a fragile heart of glass?
who would take my rejected heart
and never let it break in half?

if you only knew what you did to me. if you only knew how much pain and trauma you've caused in my life. if you only knew the amount of nights i've spent crying, and the amount of days i couldn't get myself to eat something. i really wish you knew. i really wish i could force you to be in my shoes for one day, for you to understand what you've done.

- *when vengeance conquers your mind*

it's taking everything in me to not tell you that i miss you. to not tell you that i still love you. to not tell you that i want to be with you again. every time we talk hurts a little bit more, because i have so much on my chest that i want to get rid of, but i know i can't. i have so much to tell you because there's so much going on in my life, and i just can't. i thought the pain would stop by now, but it's been so many months and there's still no end in sight.

and how i wish that i could send you this, but i can't. i'm sure you've moved on, it's been quite a while, but it seems like i'm still stuck on the memories of the past. i can't shake the thought of you and of us off my body and mind. i simply can't forget you.

my emotions
feel like a rollercoaster
i want to be happy
but i'm comfortable being sad
but i also despise being sad
it's like i'm stuck in a hole
rejecting everyone
who's trying to help me
who's trying to get me out of it

tulips and forget-me-nots

our love
was like a rollercoaster
full of ups and downs
we held tight on to the belief
that it was made up of more ups than downs
we pretended to be blindfolded
so we couldn't see
the amount of downs
and how deep they were in reality

for some time
you pulled my self-esteem down
made me feel
like you left because i wasn't enough
beautiful enough
smart enough
funny enough
enough for you to love me

i spent nights
thinking how i could be enough for you
enough for someone else
i wish i knew
that i only had to be enough
for myself

tulips and forget-me-nots

i was in a place
where i didn't even get the bare minimum
begging for time and affection
asking for flowers
just for my words to fly next to your ears
i thought it was normal
i thought that i was asking for too much
that you may have just forgotten
about the things i've begged you to do

i know now that there is a place
out there for me
where i won't have to mention
any of these things
and still get them without second-thinking
where i'll be appreciated and loved
the way i deserve to be

when have you had enough? when do you stop and realize that this isn't what you deserve? that you aren't treated the way you should? when do you start realizing that there's so much better out there? so many people you haven't met, so much love that you'll still give and receive?

it isn't the end of the world

tulips and forget-me-nots

and the home you had in my heart
turned into ashes
after you set our love on fire

between two lovers
one of them will always
love a little more
care a little more
dream about the future a little more
hope a little more
appreciate a little more

i'll always be that person
and it frustrates me
why do i keep giving so much of myself
without having it reciprocated?
why do i keep choosing people
who won't choose me back?

tulips and forget-me-nots

i've never loved someone in my life
as much as i've loved you
and i've never felt so unloved by anyone
the way you made me feel

sometimes i ask myself
what would be if we had never met
if i would have a bigger smile on my face
or if i would have found my true love yet
maybe i'd be happier now
with another person by my side
who chose to stay
and not leave when things got rough

my heart may have never been broken
i may have never been in pieces
i wouldn't need stitches now
or bandaids to cover the bruises

that's why i sometimes wish
i had never met you
because despite giving me the best memories
you took them all away, too
as if they had meant nothing to you

that's why sometimes i wish
that you had never meant something to me
because i wouldn't need to learn now
how to live without you

tulips and forget-me-nots

we disappeared from each other's lives fast
like waves disappear
the moment they hit the shore
we disappeared
the moment the true love started
without even realizing it

crazy
how we turned into strangers
who once passionately loved each other
crazy
how it ended up
being the better solution in your eyes
the better solution to let me go
instead of fixing it and building the life
the life we promised each other
the life we dreamt of
crazy
how crazy you were about me once
and how indifferent you are now

tulips and forget-me-nots

should i have just held on a little longer?
would we be happy if had sent that text?
would we have come out stronger
or would i still be moving on to the next?

because the truth is
that i held as tight as i could
on to such a thin rope
that still connected our hearts
but my grip
was slowly getting weaker
and i think that the only solution
was cutting that rope
in two halves
cutting whatever still connected us
cutting you out of my life
cutting myself free from you

the thought of you
still angers me once in a while
still leaves me wondering
if there was nothing left to save

it's exhausting
to have to think about you
day and night

i know that i should delete your number. i know that i should get rid of our pics together. i know that i should erase our conversations. but that would mean that it's the end, and maybe part of me doesn't want to get rid of the last memories that i still have of you.

because what if we never get to make more memories together in the future? what if i want to remember you one day, but won't have anything that reminds me of you?

- i don't want to forget you

it feels weird to know that i don't exist in your life anymore and to not have you in mine. to not know if you're happy or feel lonely. to not know what you're doing every day. although i know all your dreams and all the things you want to achieve in your life, i have no idea if you are pursuing them or if maybe you've changed your mind.

it feels so weird to know all the intimate parts of you, every emotional scar of yours, every single one of your secrets. to know your entire life, all the things that you went through. and it's so weird that you know everything about me too without existing in each other's lives.

i guess that's what happens when you stop watering love. it never blooms again.

the soulmate i once saw in you
turned into a stranger
whom my heart
can't recognize anymore

i'm not scared of you never coming back to me. i know that if it's meant to be, it eventually will. if it's meant to be, you'll be part of my life again.

but i'm scared of our hands not feeling the same warmth when they hold each other. our fingers not intertwining like they once used to. feeling like i'm kissing a stranger when i put my lips on yours. i'm scared of having forgotten your persona, and my body and mind not wanting to remember you. i am scared that you're not even a memory to my heart anymore.

i'm not scared of you never coming back to me. but when you do, i fear that my heart won't want to recognize you anymore, and i'll be left with a stranger, who i can't love the way i once used to.

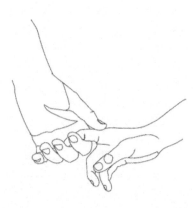

why did you ask me
to leave my door open for you
if you weren't planning
on setting foot on my doorstep again?

the healing

sometimes
the absence of people
gives us the closure we need

i felt your absence in my life
to the fullest
but after a while i found my peace

i am no longer waiting for you
no longer hoping you'll come back

what's meant to be will be
and we were certainly not that

and one day
you'll wake up in the morning
and look out the window
you'll realize that the flowers are still blooming
the sun is still shining
and the earth is still spinning
you'll look into the mirror
and instead of dreading what you could see
you'll finally be enchanted
with your own reflection
one day
the journey will finally make sense
and instead of feeling half-hearted
you'll feel whole again

don't give up yet

i hope you realize
how lucky the world is to have you in it
how lovable you are
and that your big heart
deserves to be cherished
by everyone who enters it

i hope you realize
that falling down
only means that you'll get up stronger
and that you have the capability
to shine brighter than the sun

i hope you realize
that some people don't deserve you
and that they aren't worth the pain
that they put you through

i hope you'll realize your worth someday
and that you won't let anyone
ever take it away from you

your heart has so much love to give, do
yourself a favour and keep some of it.

if there is something you taught me
after leaving me broken
it's that i'm not a 'just in case'
or a 'maybe someday'
i'm not someone
who will sit around
waiting for you to realize
what you had in first place
i am all or nothing
no middle ground
and certainly not an uncertainty
waiting to be chosen by someone
by someone who isn't sure about me
who doesn't see the unique shine in my eyes
that i am sure the right person
would immediately notice

my heart deserves to get the love
that i give to everyone else in my life
because i am tired of regretting loving people
who only show up to break my heart

thank you
for helping me get rid of someone
who didn't feel lucky enough
to have me by their side

it wasn't easy
to heal after you left
it wasn't easy
to act like we've never met

i hate that i had to erase
all the memories of you
but only the ones in my mind
because i still kept the pictures of us two

tulips and forget-me-nots

my foolish heart
loved you until it couldn't anymore
i had to give up on you
the same way you gave up on me

i've always had a habit
of making my happiness
depend on other people
i was overthrown by sadness
the moment x or y left my life

but i can't let people
choose my emotions
i can't have a person
be responsible for making me happy
it's unfair to them
and it's especially unfair to me

i need to know
how to be happy by myself
chase happiness on my own
adore my own company
and not be bothered
by people coming and going

tulips and forget-me-nots

never forget:

your worth isn't defined by their love for you

you don't need to prove yourself to anyone

the right person will make sure your heart
doesn't ache for them

you deserve genuine love

choose people who choose you back

sometimes
we hold on to the wrong people
on to false memories
on to dead memories

sometimes
we romanticize things we shouldn't
things that broke us apart

sometimes
we need to give ourselves a little bit of credit
for all the work of moving on

it's better to have loved and lost, than never to have loved at all. that's what they always say, no? but i don't think that it's a loss. i may not have you anymore, but i found myself again. i got a better version of myself in exchange, the version of me that will never leave. the version of me that will always be full of self-love and confidence. so i don't think that i lost anything at all, while you lost the best you could ever get.

there was a before you, there was a during you, and even if it's the last thing i've wanted, there will be an after you. there will be an after you, where my soul will be happy again, where my smile will be genuine and where i'll live life to the fullest again. there will be an after you, where i won't grieve you anymore. there will be an after you, where the thought of you won't drain me out anymore, and where my pillows won't be soaked as i fall asleep.

i will never forget you and i may never stop loving you, but there will be an after you, where i will give some of that love to someone else. an after you, where i will get that same love back. and i can't wait for that *after you*.

Disclaimer: inspired by Colleen Hoover

good luck finding someone
who would have fought for you no matter what
like me
good luck finding someone
with a pure heart
that had an endless amount of love for you
like me
good luck finding someone
who would have gone
through thick and thin with you
without second thoughts
like me
good luck finding someone
who would have never left you
like me

- *too much sacrifice for the wrong person*

tulips and forget-me-nots

i think that i need to thank you

thank you for showing me what love shouldn't
feel like

thank you for showing me that self-love is all
that matters

thank you for still trying, in your own way

thank you for forcing me to improve myself

thank you for loving me at my worst

thank you for leaving and holding the door open
for the right person to enter through it

you are worth everything

you are worth sincere effort
you are worth genuine sacrifice
you are worth the bloodiest fight
you are worth the tears and the pain
you are worth the most passionate love
the type of love that never dares to stop

you are worth everything

whenever i feel down
like i'm not good enough
for you
for anyone
feeling that i don't deserve love
i think of all the battles
that i've already fought
and how despite losing some
i've always gotten up and carried on

sometimes there are days
when i'm more than content with my life
i feel loved
appreciated
cared for
but then there are also days
when i overthink everything
believe that i'm on my own
believe that i'll always be the second option
to everyone
no matter how hard i try

- healing is a fluid process

after you left me
i felt ugly
unlovable
uncherished
undeserving
but that's exactly what made me realize
that i'm beautiful
despite my flaws, i'm beautiful
despite my bad habits, i'm beautiful
even if i loathe parts of myself, i'm beautiful
even if not everyone may agree on that
i'm still beautiful
no matter what you think of me
i'll always believe i'm beautiful

tulips and forget-me-nots

sometimes
the people we love the most
hurt us the most

but never regret loving them
and giving them your all
it only proves
your big heart and kindness
and it taught you
to give it to another person
the right person
who will lock that love up
and never give the key to it away

you can't hurt me anymore
i've built a shield around my heart
a shiny armour
that only lets you know
that you messed up

in the end
we only have ourselves
we think we know a person
like the palm of our hand
just for them to remind us
that we purposely acted color blind
doing everything to ignore their true colors
that they're someone we don't recognize
after only fantasizing about who they could be
in the end
we are the only ones
able to unconditionally love ourselves
the only ones who stick by our side
when everyone else leaves
and the only ones
deserving of our profound love
and everything that we carry in our hearts

you break your own heart
waiting for them to come back

they won't come back
while you're still broken
they won't come back to someone
who is desperately running after them
suffocating them

and i know it hurts
i know it's heartbreaking
because you put so much effort into this
because you wanted to fight so badly
because you truly wanted it to work out
but you need to love yourself first
before you can love them again

holding the door open
is the worst feeling to exist
not being able to delete our memories
'just in case'
not being able to get rid of your belongings
'just in case'
not being able to talk to other people
'just in case'
not being able to fully let you go
'just in case'

- *sabotaging myself*

they allegedly always come back, don't they?

but if i had sat around
waiting for you to come back
i would have never healed
and gotten up from the ground

i would have never found my joy again
the lost spark in my eyes
i would have never opened my heart once more
but instead locked it up

so they may come back
at some point in your life
but you need to live without them, too
and choose to take care of your heart

maybe right now
you need to be alone for a while
you need to learn
how to love your own heart
and how to cherish it
before you risk
giving it away to another person

stop looking for *the one*. stop searching for the perfect person, who will presumably give you the most love and security you'll ever get. stop killing yourself by thinking that you're not deserving of love or that you're unlovable. the right one, the right love, will find you when you least expect it. when you may not even want it. when you might even reject it, simply because the thought of it makes everything inside you shudder. it will come so unexpected, out of the bluest blue and turn your life upside down and downside up. but exactly that love will make sense and you'll understand why nothing before worked out, i promise.

maybe
we weren't even meant to last
maybe you had to be the protagonist
in the story of my life
just for a while
just until i can turn into the protagonist myself
just until i am capable of writing the story myself
just until i know how to be by myself
just until i can love myself
more than i loved you

feelings fade
people come and go
pinky promises are broken
but from it we also grow

maybe we were meant to cross paths
but not follow the same way together
and that's okay

sometimes
we need to lose a person
to see what we really need
to realize that it's definitely not them

i still know your favorite song
and which band can make you cry
i still know your biggest fears
and what your future holds so bright
i still know what makes you laugh
and to which things you could never say goodbye
i still know all your obsessions
passions and what brings a twinkle in your eye
i still know you in and out
and the thought of it makes me want to cry

it's weird
how you can know a stranger
better than you know yourself

you were never the love of my life. no one deserves to get the amount of love i have to give, other than me. i am the love of my life, no one else, and especially not you.

and that gives me so much peace. because at least i know that this type of love is unconditional.

letting go
shows so much self-love
it shows so much self-respect

so even if you may have lost
someone you wanted forever
you gained so much back
your true self who stays forever

tulips and forget-me-nots

letting go
is a true blessing

imagine showing so much strength
by letting that one person go
who once meant everything to you
by being able to say no
to someone you never wanted to leave

they were never yours to begin with

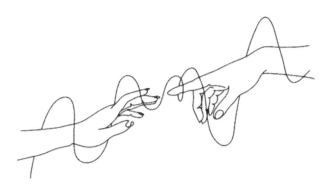

sometimes
i find myself alone at night
wondering
if maybe we had to lose sight of one another
if our paths had to split
in order to find each other again
when we're both ready
at a later point in life

sometimes
i find myself pondering
the way you left me
the way you tore me apart
and it leaves me wondering
if it had to lead to me becoming stronger
so we could be healthy again together
at a later point in life

there is beauty in pain. there is something beautiful about feeling such intense emotions for somebody, feeling so much love. it's what makes us human, it's what makes strong people stand out from the crowd.

there is beauty in the simple things in life that i experience without you, whether it's drinking my coffee in the morning or going for a walk in the evening. but they remind me of how it could be way better to experience them with you. they still remind me of the pain i felt when you left my life without saying goodbye, nor looking back on what you left behind.

you can be healed
and still wish for them to come back
still look at your phone once in a while
and unconsciously hope
that a notification from them will pop up
you can be healed
but still miss the ache once in a while
because for a long time
it was the only thing that made you feel alive
you can be healed
and still remember every part of them
as if they had never left

they will always be embedded in your heart
little pieces embracing your veins
so although you're healed
no one can tear those memories out

tulips and forget-me-nots

but the good part about healing is
that despite still wishing for them
to love you like they once used to
you know at the bottom of your heart
that you don't even need them

and maybe someday
they are capable of putting in the effort
and try to conquer your heart again
but you also know
that you deserve the world
and that at one point in life
they weren't willing to give it to you

one day, you'll miss me
you'll miss me when you're lonely
and need someone to wrap you
around their arms
you'll miss me when you have no one to talk to
and remember how i always had an open ear
you'll miss me when you start waking up
without any notification from anyone
and remember every 'good morning' i sent
you'll miss me whenever you see something
that reminds you of the way i loved you
you'll miss me when you realize
that i didn't want anything else from you
but your love and your time

one day, you'll miss me
but i won't be around
to fill the void in your heart
so you'll be sitting alone
in your bed that you made
wondering why you chose so wrong

and you'll keep on missing me

and i know i'll miss you too
but i love myself enough
to not let the missing take over me
i love myself enough
to know that the damage is unrepairable
and that there's no coming back from that

the person
that you miss right now
that you still love right now
that you still want in your life
that same person
proved over and over again
that they don't want you
that they don't love you
that they don't care about you
that they don't want to be with you
they abandoned you

they have your number
they know where to find you
yet they're still not returning
they're still not apologizing

so why do you still hold on to them?
wouldn't letting go hurt less?

you deserve someone who knows how to keep their promises. who doesn't throw the word *forever* around, as if it was something meaningless that no one cares about. you deserve someone who loves you with every inch of their body and soul, when you are the least lovable person on earth. who sees your imperfections as perfect freckles that make you who you are. you deserve someone, who gives you the same kind of love that your weary heart gives to everyone in your life. someone who isn't scared of the obstacles that life will throw at you two. who will cross oceans to make you happy because their favourite thing is seeing you smile. someone whom you can look into the eyes in 50 years and still see the same love you saw when you first met them.

you deserve that kind of person and more, so don't settle for less.

i wish that loving you
wouldn't feel like a mistake
and forgetting you
wouldn't feel like a relief

it's a weird feeling
wishing someone well
but also hoping that they won't be happier
with someone other than you

it's a weird feeling
hoping that they still crave you
and can't be happy without you
but also somehow
wanting them to be happy in life
wanting to see them accomplish everything
they have ever dreamed of

it's difficult to let go of what once was, isn't it? to accept that people change and that life isn't fair sometimes. to accept that we need to change too and aim for something higher. to let go of the dreams and hopes that quickly vanished into thin air.

it's scary to feel that you have to start a new life without your 'forever' person. to pick your pieces together that they left when they closed the door on you. but what's scarier is to stay in a place where you know exactly how unwanted you are and how the story will eventually end.

you know what happens when you keep letting them in? they start taking you for granted. they think that they can come and go as they please, because your heart will always have a soft spot for them. they think that they'll always have an option with you, in case nothing else works out. and just in case the grass isn't greener on the other side - because it never is - they know that you'll welcome them again with open arms.

but do you really want to be the second option? do you really want someone to play with your heart like that? to grab it and smash it against the wall and still expect you to pick up the pieces and give them back to them?

when someone doesn't want you, accept it.
don't try to prove your worth to someone
who is deaf to your words. don't try to make
someone, who wants to run into the
opposite direction, stay.

you deserve someone
who is sure of you
who won't have a single drop of doubt
that you are the one

you deserve someone
who wants you for the rest of their lives

if there is one thing
that i had to learn the hard way
it's that you cannot beg for love
you can't hold someone
who wants to escape your arms
you can't force someone's heart
to beat at the same pace as yours

begged love isn't true love

looking back
i realize that my effort wasn't truly reciprocated
that i had created a version of you in my head
who was perfect
and i kept telling myself
that i'm more than content with you

looking back
i realize that i had only imagined your love
that it was me who believed
that you loved me as much as i loved you
and that it was me who believed
that we were truly meant to be

you're breaking your own heart
by staying in a place
where you clearly don't belong
with a person
you definitely aren't meant to be with

whatever happens, happens

you loved this sentence, didn't you?
saying it over and over again
like a song on repeat
until i almost believed it, too

but fate doesn't work like that
fate doesn't wait for you
and our story isn't a video you can pause
until you're ready to resume it again

fate doesn't work like that
fate doesn't choose if the door is left open or not
it doesn't make decisions for you
and it won't tell you
which path to choose and when

fate is a ticking clock
whose hands won't just stop spinning
to freeze the time
until you're ready to continue

so no,
there is no 'whatever happens, happens'
because it is you who makes it happen
and it's you who decides
if you want to make it happen

let them go

i know the ache that this brings with it. the pain you feel in your heart caused by the thought of not having them in your life again. i know that your chest feels heavy and that the fear you feel inside is unbearable. but the thing is, they don't want to be a part of your life anymore. they've made the conscious decision to leave you and everything you've built behind and they keep choosing this every single day.

let them go

because that's exactly what they've wished for let their dreams come true

sometimes
we need to understand
that holding on
does more harm than good

it was never the way you are
that made me love you so much
it was my big heart
my huge capacity of love
my love never depended on you
and it never will

so i'm letting you go
knowing that i can love again
just as much as i loved you

i miss you,
but i deserve better

i miss you,
but i can't ever forget
the pain you've caused me

i miss you,
but i don't think you'll ever love me enough
to make this work

i miss you,
but i can't keep waiting for someone
who isn't coming back

i miss you,
and i probably will forever
but i can't hold on to you any longer

i can't destroy myself for love

i'm ready to raise the white flag between us.
i'm done fighting for you and for us. i'm
done battling with my inner demons, not
knowing which path to take. i'm done
waiting for change, believing that maybe
you'll want this again in the future. i'm done
drowning in an ocean of hope every single
day.

i'm ready to raise the white flag between us,
to at least give our story a good ending. i
don't want to hate you, but i can't love you
anymore either. my heart has been aching
for way too long, and if i keep loving you
it'll never stop.

maybe healing and moving on doesn't mean that i'll stop loving you. i probably never will. i may stop being *in love* with you, but a piece of my heart will always belong to yours.

so maybe healing is about me loving myself without you. me not needing reassurance from the people around me, in order to feel loved or appreciated. maybe healing is about accepting that there is a life without you, that can be just as beautiful as it was with you in it.

so even if i may never stop loving you, i think that it's time for me to start loving my life without you. to acknowledge the blue sky and the chirping birds, while i take myself out for a walk. to laugh hard with my friends, until my stomach starts aching and my mind forgets you for a minute. to see new places that won't remind me of you and to meet new people that you'll never get to know.

sure, it will take some time to find myself again. it will take some time for my smile to be fully mine again. but i can't keep losing myself in loving someone, who doesn't love me back. and maybe that's exactly what healing and moving on is about.

sometimes people are meant
to come into our lives
but not to stay
they are there to teach us a lesson
and how to not give
our hearts so easily away
that doesn't mean it wasn't real
that doesn't mean it wasn't true
it only means
that there will be a love even stronger after you

- *slowly letting you go*

one day maybe we'll cross paths
when we are older with our own families
perhaps we'll stop to chat
and laugh about how we turned into enemies
would you look at me
as the one who got away?
would you think about what could have been
if you had chosen to stay?

wherever you are right now, i hope you're okay. i hope you found the happiness you couldn't find with me. i hope you're out there, living and enjoying your life, achieving everything you've always wanted. i hope you're trying to make your dreams come true, and hopefully once in a while you're also thinking about me, too.

i hope that you look fondly on our time together and that the good memories stick with you. i hope you're surrounded by kind people and that you still radiate positivity wherever you go.

and i hope that you won't forget me, and all the love that i once gave you.

growing old together is now a distant dream. sometimes i can still see it in front of my eyes though. us on a rocking chair, with me on your lap, sitting on the porch of the house we've always dreamed of. our two children playing hide and seek in the garden, while we talk about our journey as a couple. laughing at the stupid arguments we've had and being relieved that we've managed to stick together and not let life tear us apart.

i still see it in front of my eyes, us two growing old together. but now it's just a distant dream that i know will never come true.

tulips and forget-me-nots

i wish i had known
that i would never see you again
i'd have hugged you so much tighter

i'd have kissed you goodbye
several times
enjoying each one of them
a little bit more

i would have looked you in the eyes
and remembered every single detail of your face
even though i already knew all of it by heart

i wish you had told me
that i would never see you again

dear stranger

i think that you were the longest and most beautiful chapter in my life. a chapter that i did not want to end, but we ran out of ink this time and couldn't continue writing more in the book of our love. i hope you know that this isn't how i wanted our story to end. to be honest, i didn't want it to end at all. i hope you know that i was willing to stay by your side through the good and the bad, like we always used to say. i wanted to be there for you forever, love and protect your heart until death do us apart. it saddens me that this isn't what you wanted, so i hope you find your happiness by someone else's side. i loved you dearly, and a part of me always will. but i no longer hope that our paths will cross once more in the future.

dear me

i'm proud of how far you've come. i'm proud that despite the sobbing in your pillow at night and holding tears back when you were out with friends you still managed to find peace within yourself. i believe that it can only get better from here. healing was a rocky journey and i think we're not at the point where we've completely moved on, but we're getting there. i know that one day you'll find the person who will hold you tightly in their arms and never let you go. you will smile as you lay your head on his chest and feel as content as someone can feel.

but until then, remember that happiness comes from within, and that it's not another person's job to keep you happy. there's something about being able to enjoy time with yourself that makes life a little bit better. and there's nothing wrong with being on your own.

this ends the way it started; two strangers, a little bit lost on their way, but carrying hope in their hearts. hope of finding happiness and their 'forever' person at some point, in a world in which meeting people and falling apart has always been written in the stars. with hope of finding what's meant to be.

Follow along:

Instagram: @belahpoetry
TikTok: @belahpoetry

Made in the USA
Las Vegas, NV
26 December 2023

83516501R00100